Extinct Monsters

Tasmanian Tiger

by Janet Riehecky

Reading Consultant:
Barbara J. Fox
Reading Specialist
North Carolina State University

Content Consultant:
Dr. Richard Gillespie
Visiting Fellow, Department of Archaeology and Natural History
Australian National University, Canberra

Capstone
press®

Mankato, Minnesota

Blazers is published by Capstone Press,
151 Good Counsel Drive, P.O. Box 669, Mankato, Minnesota 56002.
www.capstonepress.com

Library of Congress Cataloging-in-Publication Data
Riehecky, Janet, 1953–
    Tasmanian tiger / by Janet Riehecky.
    p. cm.—(Blazers. Extinct monsters)
    Summary: "Simple text and illustrations describe Tasmanian tigers, how
they lived, and how they became extinct"—Provided by publisher.
    Includes bibliographical references and index.
    ISBN-13: 978-1-4296-0118-4 (hardcover)
    ISBN-10: 1-4296-0118-3 (hardcover)
    1. Thylacine—Juvenile literature. I. Title. II. Series.
QL737.M336R54 2008
599.2'7—dc22   2006037696

Editorial Credits
Jenny Marks, editor; Ted Williams, designer; Jon Hughes and
    Russell Gooday/www.pixelshack.com, illustrators;
    Wanda Winch, photo researcher

Photo Credits
Nature Picture Library/Dave Watts, 29 (Tasmanian tiger)
Shutterstock/Evan Enbom, 26–27 (paddock and background); Geoffrey Jewett,
    cover (nighttime background); N Joy Neish, 26 (windmill); Ronald
    Sumners, 24–25 (Australian outback)

1 2 3 4 5 6 12 11 10 09 08 07

For Josh, with love from Aunt Janet.

Table of Contents

Chapter 1
Ancient Australia 4

Chapter 2
Weird and Wild................... 10

Chapter 3
Top Tiger 18

Chapter 4
A Monster Disappears 24

Glossary 30
Read More................................. 31
Internet Sites............................. 31
Index 32

Ancient Australia

About 30 million years ago, a weird, fierce beast prowled the wild lands of Australia.

The strange beast had a strong, lean body. It looked like a mix of tiger, wolf, and kangaroo.

The Tasmanian tiger was a top predator. This mysterious creature was one of the very largest meat-eating marsupials.

Monster Fact

Scientists named the Tasmanian tiger "Thylacine cynocephalus." The name means "pouched dog with a wolf's head."

Weird and Wild

The Tasmanian tiger had a wolflike body and soft, light brown fur. Dark brown stripes stretched across its back. Its long, stiff tail did not wag.

Tasmanian tigers were
2 feet (.6 meters) tall and
4 feet (1.2 meters) long.
They weighed about
65 pounds (30 kilograms).

Monster Fact

The Tasmanian tiger's bark sounded like a short, husky cough.

The Tasmanian tiger had a strong jaw that opened an amazing 120 degrees. When their mouths snapped shut, their 46 sharp teeth cut like scissors.

Tasmanian tigers usually gave birth to litters of three pups. The blind, hairless pups stayed in their mother's belly pouch until they were a few months old.

Tasmanian tigers dined on small animals like birds, wombats, and wallabies. Some scientists think groups of tigers tackled larger animals like kangaroos.

Tasmanian tigers weren't always on the prowl. They took shelter in caves, hollow logs, and thick bushes.

A Monster Disappears

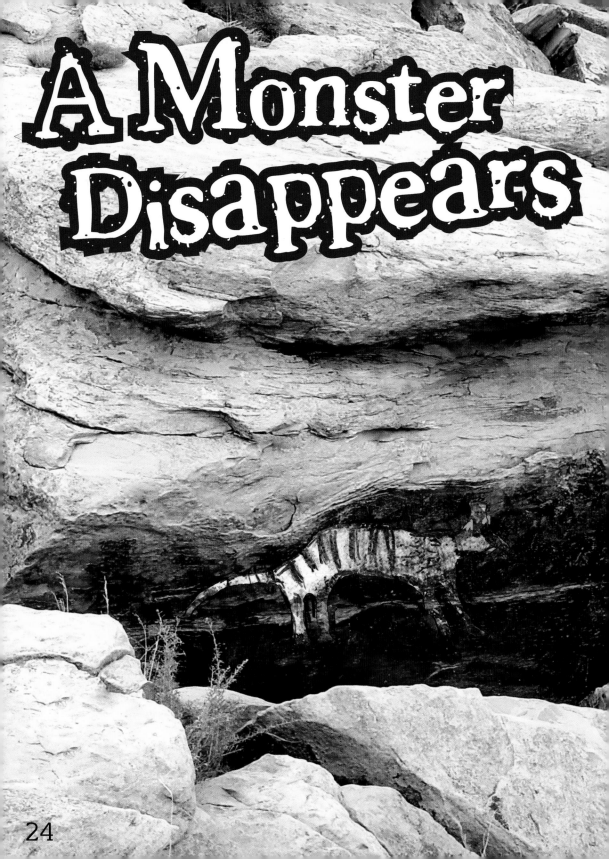

For years, Tasmanian tigers thrived in Australia. Ancient people drew pictures of these beasts on cave walls. Then, 3,000 years ago, the tigers began to disappear.

By the 1930s, tigers were only found in Tasmania, an Australian island. Ranchers there claimed tigers killed their sheep. People hunted Tasmanian tigers until none were left.

The last known Tasmanian tiger lived in the Beaumaris Zoo in Hobart, Tasmania. This animal died September 7, 1936. The tiger was named Benjamin.

Monster Fact

Scientists were unable to recreate a Tasmanian tiger by cloning one.

Benjamin

Glossary

ancient (AYN-shunt)—from a time long ago

clone (KLOHN)—to use an animal's cells to create another identical animal

litter (LIT-ur)—a group of animals born at the same time to one mother

marsupial (mar-SOO-pee-uhl)—an animal that carries its young in a pouch

pouch (POWCH)—a flap of skin that looks like a pocket in which some animals carry their young

predator (PRED-uh-tur)—an animal that lives by hunting other animals for food

prey (PRAY)—an animal that is hunted by another animal for food

prowl (PROUL)—to move around quietly and secretly

thrive (THRIVE)—to live easily and well

wallaby (WOL-uh-bee)—an Australian animal that looks like a small kangaroo

weird (WIHRD)—strange or mysterious

wombat (WOM-bat)—an Australian animal that looks like a small bear

Read More

Crew, Gary, and Mark Wilson. *I Saw Nothing: The Extinction of the Thylacine.* Sydney, Australia: Lothian Books, 2003.

Gunzi, Christine. *The Best Book of Endangered and Extinct Animals.* Boston: Kingfisher, 2004.

Internet Sites

FactHound offers a safe, fun way to find Internet sites related to this book. All of the sites on FactHound have been researched by our staff.

Here's how:
1. Visit *www.facthound.com*
2. Choose your grade level.
3. Type in this book ID **1429601183** for age-appropriate sites. You may also browse subjects by clicking on letters, or by clicking on pictures and words.
4. Click on the **Fetch It** button.

FactHound will fetch the best sites for you!

Index

Australia, 5, 25, 27

Beaumaris Zoo, 28
Benjamin, 28
bodies, 6, 11

cave drawings, 25
cloning, 29

extinction, 27, 28

fur, 11

hunting, 19, 21, 27

marsupials, 8
mouths, 15

pouches, 9, 17
predators, 8
prey, 19, 21
pups, 17

scientific name, 9
shelters, 23
size, 12

tails, 11
Tasmania, 27, 28
teeth, 15